P9-CLD-992

21st
Century
Skills Library

COOL ARTS CAREERS

FASHION DESIGNER

PATRICIA WOOSTER

CHERRY LAKE
Publishing

Published in the United States of America by
Cherry Lake Publishing, Ann Arbor, Michigan
www.cherrylakepublishing.com

Content Adviser
Clara Henry, Director, Fashion Design Program, School of Engineering and Textiles,
Philadelphia University, Philadelphia, Pennsylvania

Credits
Cover and page 1, ©CandyBoxPhoto/Shutterstock, Inc.; pages 4 and 28,
©Frances M. Roberts/Alamy; page 6, ©iStockphoto.com/CandyBoxPhoto;
page 9, ©Media Bakery; pages 10, 19, and 26, ©iStockphoto.com/talymel;
page 13, ©Levaent Konuk/Shutterstock, Inc.; page 14, ©iStockphoto.com/leezsnow;
page 15, ©Tetra Images/Alamy; page 16, ©iStockphoto.com/robcruze;
page 20, ©Image Source/Alamy; page 21, ©Nyul/Dreamstime.com; page 22,
©Dmitriy Shitonosov/Shutterstock, Inc.; pages 24 and 25, ©Lebrecht Music and Arts
Photo Library/Alamy

Library of Congress Cataloging-in-Publication Data
Wooster, Patricia.
  Fashion designer/by Patricia Wooster.
    p. cm.—(Cool arts careers)
  Includes bibliographical references and index.
  ISBN-13: 978-1-61080-131-7 (lib. bdg.)
  ISBN-10: 1-61080-131-8 (lib. bdg.)
  1. Fashion design—Juvenile literature. 2. Fashion designers—Juvenile literature.
I. Title. II. Series.
  TT507.W667 2012
  746.9'2—dc22   2011001581

Cherry Lake Publishing would like to acknowledge
the work of The Partnership for 21st Century Skills.
Please visit www.21stcenturyskills.org for more information.

Printed in the United States of America
Corporate Graphics, Inc.
July 2011
CLFA09

COOL ARTS CAREERS

TABLE OF CONTENTS

CHAPTER ONE
**UNDERSTANDING FASHION
DESIGN** 4

CHAPTER TWO
A DAY ON THE JOB. 10

CHAPTER THREE
**BECOMING A FASHION
DESIGNER** 16

CHAPTER FOUR
**A FUTURE IN FASHION
DESIGN** 22

SOME FAMOUS FASHION DESIGNERS . . . 29
GLOSSARY 30
FOR MORE INFORMATION 31
INDEX. 32
ABOUT THE AUTHOR. 32

CHAPTER ONE
UNDERSTANDING FASHION DESIGN

Excitement filled the air as bright lights lit up the stage. Young men and women walked down the runway

New York's Fashion Week gives designers a chance to show off their best work.

in beautiful clothing, capturing the audience's attention. The first show of New York City's seven-day Fashion Week celebration had begun!

New York City hosted the first Fashion Week in 1943. The show was set up to let American designers show off their collections. New York's fashion industry soon grew to become one of the largest in the world. It offered even more job opportunities than the famous fashion industry of Paris, France. In 1993, Fashion Week was moved to Bryant Park. This park is located very close to the studios of many fashion designers. The designers could actually push their fashions to the shows on clothing racks. But the event outgrew its location as it became more popular.

On September 9, 2010, the fashion industry and media gathered at a new location for Fashion Week. The Lincoln Center for the Performing Arts offered more space for the 10,000 people who attended each day. This runway show is held twice each year. It is the most important fashion event in the country. More than 100 fashion designers show off their collections during the week. Celebrities, models, buyers, and the media all attend.

Technology plays an important part at fashion events. Runway shows, interviews, and news are recorded for **streaming** video. People at home can view these video clips on the Internet. This helps fashion designers reach new audiences.

Fashion designers create the clothing, shoes, and accessories that people wear every day. They may produce several collections each year. Usually there is a new collection for each season. Designing clothes is a long process. It can take about 6 months to go from a designer's first sketches to a finished **garment**. Many people are involved in this process. Each one specializes in a different part of the job.

Fittings allow designers to make sure their garments will look good on real people.

Pattern makers bring a fashion designer's vision to life. They turn the designer's sketches into a paper pattern. This takes great skill. A three-dimensional sketch must be converted into a two-dimensional pattern. Pattern makers need math skills to do this. They must also be familiar with sewing and **draping**. The pattern is used to create the first sample of the garment.

Cutters use the paper pattern to cut fabric into the right shapes. They have to pay attention to the design on the fabric to make sure the edges will line up when they are sewn together. Many designers use expensive fabrics, so cutters must be careful to avoid mistakes. New designers are often on tight budgets. They may only have enough money to purchase just enough fabric to complete the samples. When the cutter is done, the cut pieces are bundled and ready for sewing.

Sample sewers assemble the cut pieces and sew the first sample of the design. Once the sample is sewn, it is time for a fitting. At a fitting, live models wear the clothes for the first time. The designer may decide to make changes after seeing what the garment looks like on a real person. A pair of pants may need to be shortened. A fabric color or **texture** might need to be changed. A fitting could take 20 minutes or several hours. It depends on the number of changes the designer wants to make. One garment may need several fittings for the designer to get it right. After the sample sewer makes the changes, the garment is sent out for production.

21ST CENTURY CONTENT

Haute couture (French for "high fashion") clothing is custom-made using a person's specific measurements. A lot of work goes into creating a single garment. One dress can take more than 1,000 hours of work if there is a lot of detail. Everything is sewn by hand. Haute couture clothing is considered art.

In the last 20 years, designer clothing has become more accessible to the average person. Many designers now have lower-priced clothing lines at major chain stores. Do you think this will cause the haute couture business to grow or get smaller? Why?

Fashion designers enjoy being creative. They get to work with many different people. Every day is different. They are always working on new collections and designing for different seasons. How would you like to see a shirt you designed in a clothing store? Or on a person walking down the street? Maybe somebody famous will wear your designs someday!

Fashion designers pay attention to even the smallest details on their garments.

CHAPTER TWO
A DAY ON THE JOB

Nick works for a large design company in New York City. It designs clothing that is sold in department stores and **boutiques** around the world.

Designers can get ideas for fabrics by looking at large books of samples.

Nick is a fashion designer. He has been working in the industry for 30 years. He spends every day doing something different. A mood board hangs on the wall of his office. A mood board contains photos, sketches, and color samples that show a designer's ideas for a clothing collection. For example, a mood board could show a photograph of a painting, some fabric samples, and a sketch of a dress. Every clothing collection has its own mood board to serve as inspiration.

Nick chooses the fabric for each item of clothing. He meets with a fabric source to see its selections. He makes his choices based on color, texture, quality, and price. He might need many different fabrics for a single collection.

Nick has to stay very organized. He completes five clothing collections every year. He usually works on several clothing lines at one time. In addition, he participates in New York's Fashion Week every spring and fall. He creates about forty items for each runway show. Each show gets its own mood board. This helps Nick make sure each collection has a different theme.

Over lunch, Nick might meet with a buyer for a department store or clothing boutique. Buyers meet directly with designers to purchase clothing for their stores. They look for quality items that will sell quickly. A buyer for a store in a warm place such as Florida or California might purchase more clothing from Nick's summer collection and less clothing from the fall collection.

LIFE & CAREER SKILLS

Many people today are concerned about how clothing is made. Some clothing companies save money by using **sweatshops** to make their clothes. People may work more than 80 hours a week in unsafe environments. They are paid very little for their work. Recently, many designers have stopped using sweatshops because of the poor working conditions.

The debate over clothing production is not simple. Workers lose jobs if designers stop using a particular factory. Whose responsibility is it to make sure workers are treated fairly? What can fashion designers do to improve the working conditions in clothing factories?

Clothing is advertised in magazines and on the Internet. Advertising allows designers to create an image for their **brand**. One brand name may be associated with comfort, while another may be known for being very stylish. Think of some of your favorite clothing brands. How would you describe each one?

Most clothing is made in large factories, but some is carefully made by hand.

Nick's brand represents the American lifestyle. Many of the photographs for this brand show young men and women playing sports or lounging by pools. Nick sometimes chooses the photographers who take these pictures. He might also pick the clothes, hairstyles, and locations for a photo shoot.

Sometimes fashion designers visit retail stores. Many people like to meet the designers and get fashion tips. The designers answer questions and show people how to wear their clothing.

Visiting clothing stores allows designers to share new ideas with their customers.

Photo shoots are an important part of advertising new fashions.

CHAPTER THREE

BECOMING A FASHION DESIGNER

Fashion design is a competitive business. You'll need a lot of skills if you want to succeed. You can begin learning many

You can start practicing your design skills by sketching out ideas for pieces.

of these skills now. Practice drawing sketches of clothing that you might like to make. Learn how to sew, become good at pattern making, and be sure to brush up on your math. Fashion designers use math to figure out sizes, measure fabric, and make patterns. It is also important for designers to stay up to date on technology.

Designers spend a lot of time learning about fashion **trends**. Educate yourself about design history, and read about the future of design. Create a list of designers and styles you like. Do you prefer classic styles or newer ones? Experiment with your own clothing styles. You can start setting trends right now!

A **portfolio** is a great way to show off your work. Include sketches of the clothing you have designed. Attach a sample of the fabric you used and a photograph of the finished product. You can organize your portfolio by fashion collection or style of clothing. Practice creating a portfolio by cutting pictures out of magazines and trying to re-create the designs.

You will need a college degree to make it in the fashion industry. Hundreds of colleges and universities offer accredited associate or bachelor's degrees in art and design. In addition to courses in sewing and fashion, many students take courses in **merchandising** and marketing. This allows them to learn both the artistic and business sides of the industry.

LEARNING & INNOVATION SKILLS

Fashion Group International (FGI) is a nonprofit organization with more than 5,000 members. It helps people in the fashion industry advance their careers and continue their education. FGI offers a directory of job postings, trend reports, and fashion archives for professionals and students. Fashion events are listed, and FGI members often receive discounts on admission. Students can also find information on career days and design competitions.

An **internship** is a great way to increase your knowledge and experience. Interns might spend some days running errands. Other times, they may be asked to help with the design process. They meet people in the fashion industry and learn to work as part of a team. Internships allow future designers to gain professional experience and learn new skills outside the classroom.

There is a lot of competition for jobs in the fashion industry. Many people are attracted to the creativity and status of the job. There are very few positions available, so potential designers have to make themselves stand out.

Internships offer students a chance to learn from professional designers.

The average salary for a fashion designer is $61,160 per year. Earnings vary based upon experience, location, and the type of job. Average pay for managers of fashion design companies is $72,560. Someone who works in a specialized design position can expect to earn about $59,560 a year. Freelance designers may earn more than the average salary, but they can never be sure if there will be work in the future.

In addition to creativity, a fashion designer needs to know how to work as part of a team. Deadlines are often tight, and long hours may be needed to finish a project. Designers also need strong communication skills to work with suppliers, clients, and coworkers.

Working well with other people is an important skill for most fashion designers.

Designers must be organized and learn to manage their time well.

CHAPTER FOUR
A FUTURE IN FASHION DESIGN

The fashion design industry is likely to change over the next few years. People want stylish clothing at low prices. Designers are using technology to make clothing faster and

Many people are interested in designer clothing.

cheaper. Their clothes are appearing in more stores and at lower prices. This trend has brought designer clothing to new audiences.

Technology has changed the way everyone does business. Cell phones and the Internet let people communicate quickly and easily. Designers can instantly send pictures of their work to people around the world. Employees in different locations can work together on the same project. This allows designers to work faster and take on several projects at once. Many designers now offer perfumes, shoes, accessories, and home goods in their product lines.

LIFE & CAREER SKILLS

Many fashion designers use technology to help them with their work. Computer-aided design (CAD) software is used to design, store, and create pattern sizes. Computer graphics tablets let designers sketch their drawings into the software with a digital pen. Designers can then use the software to view designs and make changes before patterns are cut.

In the past, designs always started with a sketch on paper. Do you think technology will replace this way of doing things or add to it? Why?

Many designers now **collaborate** with big chain stores. Isaac Mizrahi became one of the first high-end designers to do this when he created a line for Target. His line of clothing, accessories, and home goods made $300 million per year. Designer Vera Wang is best known for the wedding gowns she makes for Hollywood's biggest stars. But in 2007, she started an affordable line of clothing and accessories under the name Simply Vera. This line is sold at the budget-friendly Kohl's department stores. High-end designers are becoming household names.

Designer Isaac Mizrahi helped change the fashion industry with his products for Target stores.

Vera Wang has been designing wedding gowns for more than 20 years.

Many designer labels are now owned by large corporations. For example, Liz Claiborne Incorporated owns the Dana Buchman, Ellen Tracy, and Kate Spade clothing lines. These corporations have more resources to promote and grow a company than smaller design houses do.

One day your designs could end up on runways at big fashion shows.

Fashion design will continue to become more business-minded than it once was. Smaller design houses are disappearing, and corporations are taking over. Most designers can expect to work in larger teams and be involved in more product lines.

No matter how the industry changes, people will always love clothing. Fashion designers will continue to create new trends and styles. They will combine technology with traditional methods to produce their work. Will you join the exciting world of fashion design?

LEARNING & INNOVATION SKILLS

Fashion designers use social media to promote their clothing. Designers can photograph models wearing their designs and post the pictures online. People can comment on the outfits, send the photos to another Web site, or e-mail them to a friend. This is a great way for designers to generate publicity and increase traffic on their Web sites. Social media outlets such as Facebook, Twitter, and blogs help designers build a following for their clothing.

Ralph Lauren is known around the world for his classic American designs.

SOME FAMOUS FASHION DESIGNERS

Coco Chanel (1883–1971) was a fashion designer who invented the "little black dress" and created timeless suit jackets. Today her legacy continues under the direction of designer Karl Lagerfeld. Numerous books and films have been produced about her contributions to the fashion industry.

Ralph Lauren (1939–) creates clothing and home goods that combine comfort with an East Coast preppy look. In 1972 he designed a casual short-sleeve shirt available in a wide variety of colors. It became known as the Polo shirt and is still Lauren's biggest seller.

Yves Saint Laurent (1936–2008) was a couture fashion designer who stressed tailoring in his collections. He is best known for creating the smoking tuxedo jacket, peasant blouses, and jumpsuits.

Oscar de la Renta (1932–) is a fashion designer best known for his formal wear for men and women. He has dressed many famous people, including actors, first ladies, and socialites.

Pamela Skaist-Levy (1964–) started the Juicy Couture clothing brand with her partner Gela Nash-Taylor. They are best known for their casual tracksuits and catchy slogans. The company has grown to include children's clothing, perfume, and handbags.

Anna Sui (1964–) was interested in fashion from a young age. She attended Parsons School of Design and had her first runway show in 1991. In 2009, she won the Council of Fashion Designers of America Geoffrey Beene Lifetime Achievement Award.

GLOSSARY

boutiques (boo-TEEKS) small specialty shops

brand (BRAND) the personality and image of a company or product

collaborate (kuh-LAB-uh-rate) to work with other people on a project

draping (DRAY-peeng) to arrange fabric in a loose and flowing way on a dress form

garment (GAR-mint) a piece of clothing

internship (IN-turn-ship) a way to gain work experience while being mentored

merchandising (MUR-chuhn-dize-eeng) making and using a sales strategy for a product

pattern (PAT-urn) a paper plan for creating, cutting, and sewing a garment

portfolio (port-FOH-lee-o) a collection of sketches and photographs that show off a fashion designer's work

streaming (STREE-meeng) sent through the Internet

sweatshops (SWET-shops) factories where workers are forced to work long hours for little pay

texture (TEKS-chur) the way something feels

trends (TRENDZ) styles that are popular for a short time

FOR MORE INFORMATION

BOOKS

Faerm, Steven. *Fashion Design Course.* Hauppauge, NY: Barrons Educational Series, 2010.

Nunnelly, Carol A., *The Encyclopedia of Fashion Illustration Techniques.* Philadelphia: Running Press, 2009.

Travers-Spencer, Simon, and Zarida Zaman. *The Fashion Designer's Directory of Shape and Style.* Hauppauge, NY: Barrons Educational Series, 2008.

WEB SITES

Fashion Group International
www.fgi.org
Learn more about fashion industry news, trends, and opportunities.

National Association of Schools of Art and Design
nasad.arts-accredit.org
Find out more about accredited art and design programs that are available.

Style.com—Fashion Shows
www.style.com/fashionshows
Discover the latest fashion trends by viewing designer runway shows.

INDEX

advertising, 12

brands, 12, 14, 29
budgets, 7
buyers, 5, 11

Chanel, Coco, 29
collections, 5, 6, 8, 11, 17, 29
communication, 20, 23
competition, 16, 18
computer-aided design (CAD), 23
Conrad, Lauren, 29
corporations, 26, 27
cutters, 7

draping, 7

education, 17, 18

fabrics, 7, 11, 17
Fashion Group International (FGI), 18
Fashion Week, 5, 11

fittings, 7
freelance designers, 19–20

haute couture clothing, 8

Internet, 5, 12, 23, 27
internships, 18, 29

labels, 26
Lauren, Ralph, 29
Lincoln Center for the Performing Arts, 5

Mizrahi, Isaac, 24
models, 5, 7
mood boards, 11

New York City, 5, 11

pattern makers, 7, 17, 23
photographs, 11, 14, 17, 23, 27
portfolios, 17

Renta, Oscar de la, 29
retail stores, 8, 11, 14, 23, 24, 29
runway shows, 4–5, 11

Saint Laurent, Yves, 29
salaries, 19–20
sample sewers, 7
seasons, 6, 8, 11
sewing, 7, 8, 17
Skaist-Levy, Pamela, 29
sketches, 6, 7, 11, 17, 23
Sui, Anna, 29

teamwork, 18, 20, 27
technology, 5, 17, 22–23, 27
trends, 17, 18, 23, 27, 29

Wang, Vera, 24

ABOUT THE AUTHOR

Patricia Wooster has a degree in creative writing and psychology from the University of Kansas. She lives with her husband and two sons in Tampa, Florida.